International Workshop on Data Mining in Marketing (DMM 2019)

New York, New York, USA
19 July 2019

Editors:

Petra Perner

ISBN: 978-1-5108-9515-7

Printed from e-media with permission by:

Curran Associates, Inc.
57 Morehouse Lane
Red Hook, NY 12571

Some format issues inherent in the e-media version may also appear in this print version.

ibai-publishing
Arno-Nitzsche-Str. 45
04277 Leipzig, Germany

info@ibai-publishing.org

Additional copies of this publication are available from:

Curran Associates, Inc.
57 Morehouse Lane
Red Hook, NY 12571 USA
Phone: 845-758-0400
Fax: 845-758-2633
Email: curran@proceedings.com
Web: www.proceedings.com

Table of Content

Petra Perner (Ed.)

Data Mining in Marketing

International Workshop on Data Mining in Marketing DMM 2019
New York, USA, July 19, 2019

Proceedings

ibai Publishing
www.ibai-publishing.org

Volume Editor

Petra Perner
Institute of Computer Vision and Applied Computer Sciences, IBaI
PF 30 11 38
04275 Leipzig
E-mail: pperner@ibai-institut.de

The German National Library listed this publication in the German National Bibliography.
Detailed bibliographical data can be downloaded from http://dnb.ddb.de.

Data Mining in Marketing DMM

Intern. Workshop on Data Mining in Marketing DMM'2019

July 19, 2019, New York, USA

Workshop Chair

Ingrid Neuhaeuser, IBaI, Germany

Workshop Committee

Seppe vanden Broucke	KU Leuwen, Belgium
Maria Ciurea,	University of Petroani, Romania
Khin Lwin	University of Nottingham, UK
Jufeng Peng	Shanghai Jiao Tong University, China
Habib Jadj-Mabrouk	French Institute of Science and Technology of Transport, Spatial Planning, Development and Networks, France
Ron Kenett	KPA, Israel
Samuel Noriega	Universitat de Barcelona, Spain
Irena Ograjensek	University Jubilianja, Slovenia
Petra Perner	Institute of Computer Vision and applied Computer Sciences, IBaI, Germany
Gero Szepannek	University Stralsund, Germany
Wouter Verbeke	Vrije Universiteit Brussel, Belgium
Bing Zhu	Business School of Sichuan University, China

Preface

The International Workshop on Data Mining in Marketing DMM was held in connection with the Industrial Conference on Data Mining ICDM and the International Conference on Machine Learning and Data Mining MLDM.

Although the number of presenters were small the audience was large. That gave the presenters the possibility to present long the talks. The discussion afterwards was long and raised a lot of issue concerned with the subject of online marketing. It gave important impulses of thing that should be considered with online marketing.

We would like to thank all reviewers for their highly professional work and their effort in reviewing the papers.

We also thank the members of the Institute of Applied Computer Sciences, Leipzig, Germany (www.ibai-institut.de), who handled the conference as secretariat. We appreciate the help and understanding of the ibai-publishing publishing house (www.ibai-publishing.org) that handled the papers and published the proceedings.

Last, but not least, we wish to thank all the speakers and participants who contributed to the success of the workshop.

We hope to see you in 2020 in New York at the next World Congress on "The Frontiers in Intelligent Data and Signal Analysis, DSA 2020" (www.worldcongressdsa.com), which combines under its roof the following three events: International Conferences Machine Learning and Data Mining MLDM (www.mldm.de) , the Industrial Conference on Data Mining ICDM (www.datamining-forum.de), and the International Conference on Mass Data Analysis of Signals and Images in Artificial Intelligence and Pattern Recognition with Applications in Medicine, Biotechnology, Chemistry and Food Industry, MDA-AI&PR (www.mda-signals.de). In connection with these conferences runs the workshop on Data Mining in Marketing DMM (http://www.data-mining-forum.de/w_marketing.php) again.

July 2019 Petra Perner

Text Classification and Sentiment Analysis in Social Media for the Marketing Domain

Yaakov HaCohen-Kerner

Dept. of Computer Science, Jerusalem College of Technology - Lev Academic Center, 9116001 Jerusalem, Israel
kerner@jct.ac.il

Abstract. The increase in online social media provides an excellent platform for companies, on the one hand, to read and learn from customers and improve their marketing policies and on the other hand, to perform various analysis and classification tasks. In this short paper, we present basic statistics of the domains of text classification, sentiment analysis, social media, and marketing over the last nine years. The three main findings derived from these statistics are: (1) the sentiment analysis, text classification, and social media topics are increasing; (2) the marketing topic is declining; and (3) marketing combined with (sentiment analysis or text classification or social media) are constantly increasing. We also reviewed a few studies relevant to these domains. We can see that in many of these studies: (1) relatively simple tasks have been performed such as simple sentiment classification (only to positive, negative or neutral without predicting the degree of the sentiment and finding the underlying causes of positive or negative sentiments); (2) relatively simple features have been applied; and (3) only SVM methods have been applied.

Keywords: Data Mining, Marketing, Sentiment Analysis, Supervised Machine Learning, Text Classification.

1 Introduction

The constant and impressive increase in online social media (e.g., Facebook, Flickr, Twitter, blogs, forums, and websites) provides an excellent platform for organizations and companies to read and learn from customers [9]. Traditional marketing methods such as face-to-face interviewing and focus groups are both costly and time-consuming, and sometimes even biased. In contrast, huge social media, such as the millions of blogs, and tweets are available for free.

Customer satisfaction and consumer complaint behavior have both been recognized in the academic and the practical world as important phenomena, which impact an organization's success [11]. The marketing policies of organizations and companies can be greatly influenced by text analysis in general, and sentiment analysis, in particular based on various natural language processing (NLP) tools and text classification, using supervised machine learning (ML) methods.

In this short paper, we present, on the one hand, basic and preliminary statistics of the domains of text classification, sentiment analysis, social media, and marketing, and on the other hand, summaries of a number of articles relevant to these domains.

The structure of this paper is as follows. Section 2 introduces some general trends of the discussed domains. Section 3 provides summaries of several relevant articles. Finally, Section 4 summarizes and offers some suggestions for future research.

2 General Trends in the Discussed Domains

In this section, we show a number of trends in the scientific research conducted in the domains of text classification, sentiment analysis, social media, and marketing. At the beginning, we decide to check these trends by the following simple heuristic method that counts the number of publications having these domains in the publications' titles, over the last nine years (2010-2018), retrieved by Google scholar's engine. Google scholar was chosen because it is a freely accessible bibliographic database, which enables web search of most online academic journals and books, conference papers, theses and dissertations, preprints, abstracts, technical reports, and other scholarly literature, including court opinions and patents[1].

Table 1 presents the number of publications having the various discussed domains in the publications' titles.

Table 1. Number of publications having the domains in the publications' titles.

Year	keywords			
	marketing	**sentiment analysis**	**text classification**	**social media**
2010	16,600	201	341	3,410
2011	20,600	301	319	6,000
2012	20,000	486	355	7,780
2013	20,200	672	337	8,650
2014	19,200	890	335	9,320
2015	20,700	1,070	381	9,940
2016	17,200	1,280	414	10,400
2017	17,000	1,500	445	10,500
2018	14,100	1,540	550	10,500

In Table 1[2], we see two main trends. The first trend is the decline of the number of publications having "marketing" in their titles over the last nine years. The second trend is the increase of the number of publications having "sentiment analysis", "text classification", and "social media" in their titles over the last nine years.

Fig. 1 presents the first trend, using a polynomial of degree five (this function was found to be most suitable for describing the trend shown in the graph from a wide range of functions of different degrees). The second trend is presented in Figures 2-4 (in these

[1] "Search Tips: Content Coverage". *Google Scholar.* Retrieved 27 April 2016.

[2] According to Google Scholar on 20-MAR-19.

figures as well, each graph was described using the function that was found to be most suitable from a wide range of functions of different degrees).

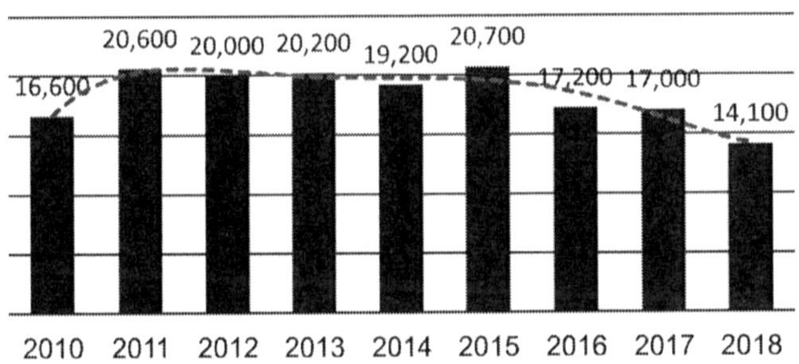

Fig. 1. # of publications in Google Scholar having "marketing" in their title for the last 9 years.

Fig. 2 presents an increase of the results over the years using a rising linear line.

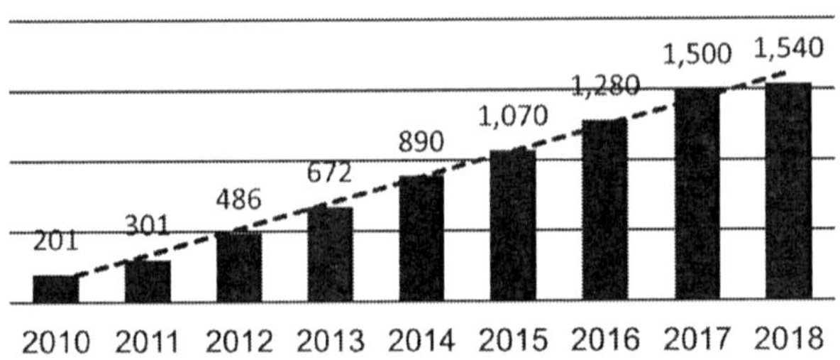

Fig. 2. # of publications in Google Scholar having "sentiment analysis" in their title for the last 9 years.

Fig. 3 presents an increase of the results over the years using a polynomial of degree six.

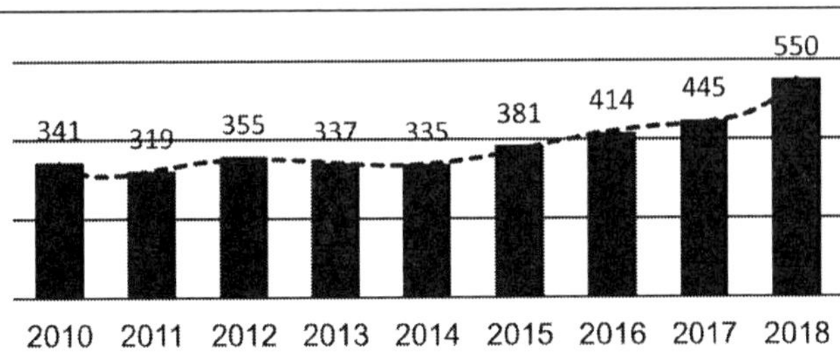

Fig. 3. # of publications in Google Scholar having "text classification" in their title for the last 9 years.

Fig. 4 presents an increase of the results over the years using a polynomial of degree two.

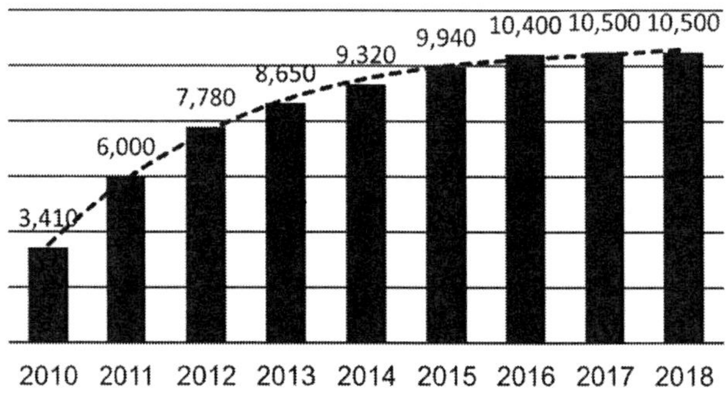

Fig. 4. # of publications in Google Scholar having "social media" in their title for the last 9 years.

On the one hand, the general trend introduced in Figure 1 shows a decline in the number of publications having "marketing" in their titles over the last nine years.

On the other hand, there is an increase of research in text classification, sentiment analysis, and social media according to Table 1 and Figures 2-4, where we see the number of publications in Google Scholar having "text classification", "sentiment analysis", and "social media" in their title for the last nine years. The overall trend in Figures 2-4 is an increase in the number of publications having "marketing" in their titles over the last nine years.

We then decided to generate a new table (Table 2) that presents the number of articles containing (anywhere in the paper) at least one appearance of "marketing" with at least one appearance of each of the other keywords, as well as creating appropriate Figures (Figures 5-7).

Table 2. Number of publications containing marketing with each of the other keywords.

Year	Concept		
	marketing & sentiment analysis	marketing & text classification	marketing & social media
2010	693	433	13,600
2011	1,180	499	22,600
2012	1,850	642	34,300
2013	2,610	680	46,700
2014	3,500	755	56,600
2015	4,550	951	56,900
2016	5,310	1,010	57,700
2017	6,480	1,160	59,000
2018	7,280	1,180	45,000

Fig. 5 presents an increase of the results over the years using a rising linear line.

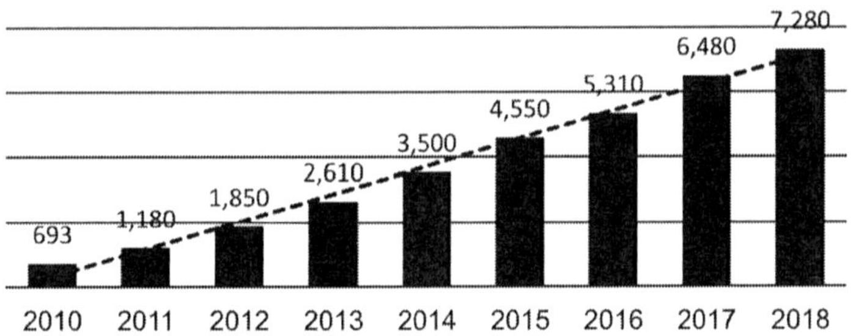

Fig. 5. # of publications in Google Scholar having "marketing" & "sentiment analysis" for the last 9 years.

Fig. 6 presents a decline of the results over the years using a rising linear line.

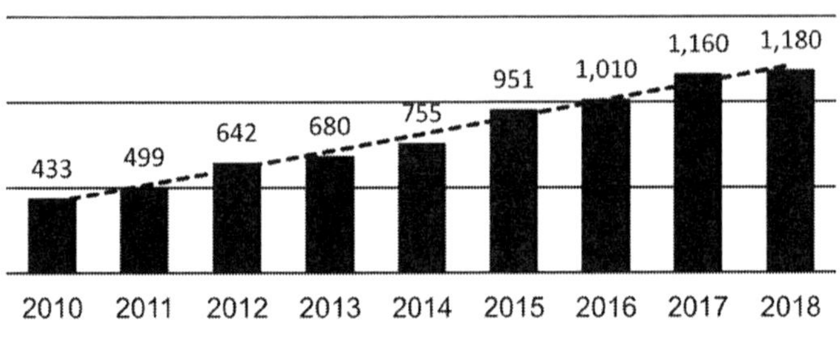

Fig. 6. # of publications in Google Scholar having "marketing" & "text classification" for the last 9 years.

Fig. 7 presents a decline of the results over the years using a polynomial of degree two.

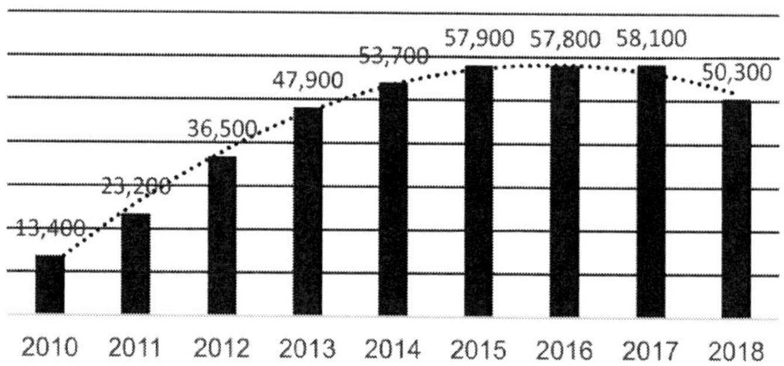

Fig. 7. # of publications in Google Scholar having "marketing" & "social media" for the last 9 years.

Figures 5 and 6 present a similar overall trend, which is a linear increase in the number of publications having "marketing" & "sentiment analysis" or "text classification" over the last nine years. Figure 7 presents the number of publications having "marketing" & "social media" over the last nine years. The general trend is a clear increase trend until 2015. During 2015-2017, the number is rather steady.

These findings show that the study of marketing combined with the other keywords is in general increasing until at least 2018. In 2018, there is an increase for two first combinations ("marketing" & "sentiment analysis", "marketing" & "text classification") and only one puzzling and unexplained decline for the "marketing" & "social media" combination. The overall picture of the increase in the number of publications of these three combinations over the years is particularly noteworthy, given the fact that "marketing" itself is declining, at least according to its frequency in the headlines of articles.

3 Previous Studies

In this section, we present a summary of a number of articles relevant to the discussed domains. Each summary contains a description of the presented research and its results. In addition, each summary will contain, as much as possible, shortcomings and/or future work that is offered for the discussed study.

Glance et al. [4] described an end-to-end system that is used to support a number of marketing intelligence and business intelligence applications, e.g., early alerting – informing subscribers when a rare but critical, or even fatal, condition occurs; buzz tracking – following trends in topics of discussion and understanding what new topics are forming; and sentiment mining – extracting aggregate measures of positive vs. negative opinion. Their system collects specific types of online content and provides analytics based on classification, NLP tools (e.g., a part-of-speech (POS) tagger and a shallow parser), phrase finding, and other mining technologies in a marketing intelligence application. The analysis system allows a user to rapidly characterize the data, to and drill down to discover and validate specific issues. The system delivers both qualitative and quantitative accounts of features derived from online messages. The authors of this article neither mentioned shortcomings of their system nor offered any suggestions for future work.

Engin and Can [2] investigated the semantic classification of Turkish Web documents in the marketing domain. They constructed various feature extraction methods, based on characteristics of the Turkish language, structures of Web documents, and online content in the marketing domain. They constructed a labeled marketing dataset in Turkish. They applied and compared various support vector machine (SVM) configurations, using the TFIDF scheme, considering the performance needs of practical context-sensitive systems. Their results show that linear kernel classifiers achieve the best performance in terms of accuracy and speed on text documents expressed as keyword root features. The authors suggest extension of their research study in two main areas. The first is to improve the feature extraction and classification phases using NLP tools such as a Turkish WordNet, Named entity recognizers, part of speech taggers and other language processing methods. The second is the design and development of the ad distribution system as a practical mechanism. Their dataset can be generalized with new labeled web documents that have different page structures and contents, and their labeling and keyword extracting procedures should be improved and made more efficient.

Cho and Kang [1] proposed a method of text sentiment classification for social network service (SNS)-based marketing for tweets written in Korean in five different datasets (Consumer Products, Persons, Travel, Food, and Movies), where each dataset contains a few hundred tweets. In contrast to previous methods that used only formal vocabulary, the authors use also informal vocabulary such as emoticons and newly coined words. They built five special sentiment-based domain dictionaries, in which each vocabulary is associated with a sentiment and its weight. The sentiment is labeled as one of three sentiments (positive, negative or neutral) if at least 7 of 10 students agreed on the label. Each tweet is decomposed into morphemes using an existing morpheme analyzer. They create a feature vector for each morpheme, using the sentiment-based domain dictionaries. They applied 10 cross-validation. The sentiment of each tweet is classified by a SVM classifier. Their method presents better performance in almost all type of measures (precision, recall, and F1-Measure) in all five examined tasks. In this research paper too, the authors neither mentioned shortcomings of their system nor offered any suggestions for future work.

Mostafa in his research [10], attempted to answer the following research questions: (1) Can social networks' opinion mining methods be used to successfully detect hidden patterns in consumers' sentiments towards global brands? and (2) Can companies effectively use the blogosphere to redesign their advertising and marketing campaigns? He used a random sample of 3,516 tweets to evaluate consumers' sentiment towards sixteen global brands, e.g., DHL, IBM, KLM, Nokia, and T-Mobile. He used an expert-predefined lexicon including about 6,800 seed adjectives with known orientation (2,006 positive words and 4,783 negative words) to perform the analysis. To conduct the qualitative part of this study, the author used the QDA Miner 4.0 software package (Provalis Research [12]). The results indicate a generally positive consumer sentiment towards several famous brands. The author noted three drawbacks of their system and proposed future research ideas to solve these drawbacks, as follows: (1) Their sentiment analysis component does not reveal the underlying reason behind the consumers' opinions. Future research using sentiment topic recognition should be conducted to determine the most representative topics discussed behind each sentiment, and by that way it should be possible to gain overall knowledge regarding the underlying causes of positive or negative sentiments. (2) Their lexicon-based approach can detect only basic sentiments, and might fail to recognize expressions used in situations such as sarcasm, irony or provocation. A possible solution might be the use of a large corpus containing such idiomatic expressions. (3) Consumers' opinions might in fact be posted by online vendors who pretend to be as real consumers. Such opinions might distort sentiments of real consumers. Future research should try to distinguish between opinions of real consumers, and opinions that reflect the position of vendors interested in selling more products or services.

Howells and Ertugan [8] proposed a model for sentiment analysis of social media network data. Their model applies fuzzy logic methods to design, create and build social bots that can analyze consumer comments in social media networks. Their model is specifically aimed at applications in consumer relationship management, customer retention, and other aspects of marketing. The social bots of this experiment were successful as follows. 27% of the user population decided to follow one of the social bot accounts. 12% of the user population mentioned at least one of the social bots in a tweet. An idea for future research is to build a highly efficient tool that will not only find a target population, but will communicate and prompt the target for more information. Such a tool can be an extremely useful in customer relationship management, as the marketer would be able to probe the user for more feedback on a particular subject.

Giatsoglou et al. [3] proposed a generic methodology for sentiment detection out of textual snippets that express people's opinions in English and Greek. Their methodology uses a SVM method and textual documents are represented by vectors that are used for training a polarity classification model. Several documents' vector representation approaches have been explored and compared, including word embedding-based, lexicon-based, and hybrid vectorizations. The competence of these feature representations for the sentiment classification task was evaluated by experiments on four datasets containing online user reviews in both English and Greek, in order to represent high and weak inflection language groups. Possible future research are, on the one hand, to conduct experiments to showcase the flexibility and the computational efficiency of their methodology and to improve the model's performance and, on the other hand, to: (a) explore new topics beyond online customer reviews, (b) consider another high inflection language and also other language specific phenomena, (c) consider other emotional lexicons for the English language, and (d) apply the methodology to big data sentiment datasets (e.g., large tweet datasets).

4 Summary and Future Work

In this short paper, we present basic statistics of the studies in the domains of text classification, sentiment analysis, social media, and marketing over the last nine years. The three main findings derived from these statistics are: (1) the sentiment analysis, text classification, and social media topics are increasing; (2) the marketing topic is declining; and (3) marketing combined with (sentiment analysis or text classification or and social media) are increasing all over the years (except marketing combined with social media for the last few years).

In addition, we provide summaries of a few relevant articles. Each summary contains not only a description of the presented research and its results, but also as much as possible, shortcomings and/or ideas for future work that are suggested for the discussed study. The summaries show some of the potential of text classification and sentiment analysis in social media to improve marketing.

We see in many of the studies that have been surveyed above: (1) relatively simple tasks have been performed, e.g., simple sentiment classification (only to positive, negative or neutral, without predicting the degree of the sentiment and finding the underlying causes of positive or negative sentiments); (2) relatively simple features have been applied; and (3) only SVM methods have been applied. Additional advanced machine learning (ML) methods such as deep learning models should be applied at least on large datasets.

The major achievements in text classification and sentiment analysis have not yet been absorbed into many of the studies in marketing intelligence and business intelligence applications.

Possible future research proposals include (1) applying more advanced sentiment methods in the domain of marketing (e.g., automatic extraction of positive and negative words using seed lists [7]); (2) extracting a summary (e.g. [5]) and keyphrases (e.g., [6]) from each document, and using these data elements; and (3) applying the most advanced supervised ML methods such as various deep learning models to match the vast amount of knowledge available in social media.

Acknowledgments. The author thanks three anonymous reviewers for their reviews and fruitful comments. Thanks also to Shalom Mashbaum for his English editing.

References

1. Cho, S. H., Kang, H. B.: Text sentiment classification for SNS-based marketing using domain sentiment dictionary. In Proceedings of the 2012 IEEE International Conference on Consumer Electronics (ICCE) (pp. 717-718). IEEE (2012).
2. Engin, M., Can, T.: Text classification in the Turkish marketing domain for context sensitive ad distribution. In Proceedings of the 24th International Symposium on Computer and Information Sciences (pp. 105-110). IEEE (2009).

3. Giatsoglou, M., Vozalis, M. G., Diamantaras, K., Vakali, A., Sarigiannidis, G., Chatzisavvas, K. C.: Sentiment analysis leveraging emotions and word embeddings. Expert Systems with Applications, 69, 214-224 (2017).
4. Glance, N., Hurst, M., Nigam, K., Siegler, M., Stockton, R., Tomokiyo, T.: Deriving marketing intelligence from online discussion. In Proceedings of the eleventh ACM SIGKDD international conference on Knowledge discovery in data mining (pp. 419-428)ACM (2005).
5. HaCohen-Kerner, Y., Malin, E., Chasson, I: Summarization of Jewish law articles in Hebrew. In CAINE (pp. 172-177) (2003).
6. HaCohen-Kerner, Y., Gross, Z., Masa, A.: Automatic extraction and learning of keyphrases from scientific articles. In International Conference on Intelligent Text Processing and Computational Linguistics (pp. 657-669), Springer, Berlin, Heidelberg (2005).
7. HaCohen-Kerner, Y., Badash, H.: Positive and negative sentiment words in a blog corpus written in hebrew. Procedia Computer Science, 96, 733-743 (2016).
8. Howells, K., Ertugan, A.: Applying fuzzy logic for sentiment analysis of social media network data in marketing. Procedia computer science, 120, 664-670 (2017).
9. Jin, J., Yan, X., Yu, Y., Li, Y.: Service failure complaints identification in social media: A text classification approach, In the Proc. of the Thirty Fourth International Conference on Information Systems (2013).
10. Mostafa, M. M.: More than words: Social networks' text mining for consumer brand sentiments. Expert Systems with Applications, 40(10), 4241-4251 (2013).
11. Pinto, M. B., Mansfield, P.: Facebook as a complaint mechanism: An investigation of millennials. Journal of Behavioral Studies in Business, 5, 1-12 (2012).
12. Provalis Research.: QDA Miner version 4.0 User Manual. Montreal, QC, Canada (2011).

Functions and Architecture for Automatic Predictive Targeting and Modelling Real-time On-line Behavior

Petra Perner

Institute of Computer Vision and Applied Computer Sciences, IBaI
PF 30 11 38, 04251 Leipzig
pperner@ibai-institut.de

Abstract. To detect fast changes in customer behavior or to react in as focused a manner as possible, predictive modeling must be done in good quality to get effective predictions of customer behavior and it has to be done fast to be relevant under business aspects. Modeling speed is of great importance in industry as time is a crucial factor. This necessity requires a different technical set up for model development to fulfill both needs: quality and development speed. Today most companies like to develop their models individually with the help of specialists. But for a lot of companies, this way takes too long; even though the models are excellent, the time to develop them sometimes kills the advantages of a better prediction. This article describes the general structure and ideas how to implement industry-focused model production that will help to react quickly to changing behavior. We will discuss the key success factors and the pitfalls of this assembly line model product.

1 Marketing in the Web 2.0

Customer profiles are really valuable if they contain more information than just customers' past behavior, but also include present reactions and give reliable predictions about their future conduct.

A company's existing customer data may, for example, provide information about purchase and payment history, address, age, gender, etc. For all customers that can be identified this data is stored and used for targeting purposes. Even if there is a technical solution enabling you to identify customers who are already known when they visit your website, you never know all the people visiting your site. But there are plenty of reasons to learn more about them and to target them as well and to do it in the same personalized way as you do with those you can identify. But the only information available is what you can filter out of the log file.

So you know which and how many pages they have seen and for how long, where they came from and much more.

To use this information each individually brings obvious advantages: With the knowledge of the typical click patterns of customers reacting similarly and the knowledge of the positioning and placement of advertising for a product which appeals to most customers you will create a big benefit. With information such as entry and exit page, or click behavior, the structuring of web sites can be continually improved and their representation can be optimized on the web. Knowledge of the origin, points to the channels, which should best be addressed by the specific target groups.

All this information put together gives a multifaceted view of customers and target groups. To measure success, in order to recognize and to identify trends, changes and new needs of the target groups early, and seize enterprise opportunities, consider off- and online market study as well as on the analysis of the volume of data existing in the enterprise reporting, data mining and market observations. On-line measures of interested parties use the clicking advice or page impressions consulted as yardsticks [2].

But nothing changed in the last years as rapidly as the use of the Internet. 10 years ago Web 1.0 offered static websites, Web 1.5 offered dynamic websites and since 2005 more users expect interactive Websites (Web 2.0). The World Wide Web develops itself constantly in large steps and Web 3.0 will start soon.

The Internet medium penetrates the market with its various application possibilities and offers world-wide access - across all society and ethnical layers. Currently 79.9% of the Germans are already on the Web. [8]

Ever more humans use the Internet ever more extensively (for search, E-Mail, forums, Blogs, Podcasting, on-line one of plays...) - briefly: The Internet is a fast, global, highly competitive marketplace. Above all, the Web is used increasingly by many customers and enterprises as a starting point for the search for services and products.

The expenditure for on-line marketing today already takes more than 19,2% [13] of the total expenditure for advertising. This will continue to rise in all industries, because this market place opens various marketing possibilities - and demands completely new marketing strategies. Medium-spreading, target-group-specific, relevantly - today must be tailored advertising best personally to each customer. For it is necessary to improve customer loyalty, facilitate the acquisition of new customers and improve the response or the conversion rate - all at very low cost advertising [3].

The current challenges facing new methodologies and technologies are, for example, the analysis of log files [14], information on the origin of the visitor, what browser he uses, which and how many pages he has viewed. The advantages are obvious: the person who knows the typical click behavior of their customers can determine with this knowledge, the positioning and placement of advertising for a product that appeals to its customers the most. With information such as exit and entry side, the structuring of web sites can be continuously improved and the representation can be optimized on the web [4].

Of exceptional value for strategic planning are reliable predictions about future developments in the behavior and needs of customers. The development of predictive behavioral targeting ensures that such predictions are placed on a statistically validated foundation.

2 Predictive Behavioral Targeting

For a company to receive exciting customer profiles, improve the relevance of its online offerings and optimize its long term online marketing ROI, it would not only need information about the historical and current habits of its customers, but also about their future conduct [5], [10], [11]. So it is important to discover patterns in customer behavior, for this we need to identify a specific user. This makes the predictive behavioral targeting.

Methods such as descriptive statistics, click-stream analysis [6], discriminant analysis, regression methods [3], decision trees, neural networks, case-based reasoning (CBR) [12], cluster analysis [1] and time series analysis are used.

Based on analysis of user profiles and user structures (such as age, lifestyle, peer group affiliations, browsing behavior) predictive models are created for future behavior [13]. For example, the decision on where to place banners which users should be shown, is based on the sites he visited or on the basis of what he's doing on these sites.

Previously contextual advertising based on the content of a website, identified content which is best suited for a display. The predictive behavioral targeting based on the users actual and past behavior, the right person for a quote with the ability to identify user profiles, which opens the way for predictive behavioral targeting relevant advertising.

Predictive targeting makes a lot and that information gain immensely in value when they are in the right place as quickly as possible in the right form ready. Fully automatic Predictive Targeting and modelling real-time of on-line behavior create for it the conditions.

3 Fully automatic Predictive Targeting and modelling real-time on-line behavior

Using the necessary algorithms for analysis in real time opens up the new fully automated predictive targeting, individual and lasting forms of communication and offers a head start by modeling the real-time online behavior.

This means an evolution step comparably from the handicraft to the production - inclusive reductions at the complexity. The classical way to build complex forecast models by hand, is in the role of "Master Workshop". But even a large staff of analysts (craftsmen) can not cope with the huge amounts of data and the high number of models- this needs a fully automated "assembly line" for prediction models.

3.1 Function

The core of the fully automatic predictive targeting system is the construction of prediction models. It includes all functionality to build with a team of analysts complex forecast models by hand ("Master Workshop") but also in a second module ("assembly line") it builds very fast fully automated simple, click-based predictive models, automatically backs up its quality and makes it available for use.

In the "assembly line" all models are calculated, which is a relatively simple task in the field of predictions (predictive modeling), for example, only the models whose target variable is a dichotomous structure (click vs. not clicked, purchased vs. not. bought, visits vs. not visited, etc.)[9]. These prediction models cover, for example, a large portion of the orders for banners and optimization behavior targeting. Special analysis such as cluster analysis, are performed by the analysis team in the "Master Workshop".

It is decided by an administrative process whether a forecast model goes in the workshop or in the assembly line to be manufactured. Each model receives a clear ID and is archived. The substantial elements the assembly line contains are shown in Figure 1.

Modules of the Automatic Targeting System

- **Control**
  - Administration
  - Model Management
  - Management of the Variables
- **Learning of the Model**
  - Selection of the Target Variable =1 and Selection of the Target Variable=0
  - Model specific random sampling to obtain a data set
  - Supply of a Learning Data Set and aTest Data Set
  - Learning the Model
  - Evaluation of the Model
  - Quality Assurance Monitor
  - Release process
  - Handing over process
- **Model examination**
  - Model specific random sampling to obtain a data set
  - Model examination
  - Quality Assurance Monitor
  - Confirmation process
- **Model Archive**
- **Variable processing and Supply**

Fig. 1. The Elements of an Assembly Line

3.2 Architecture

The areas of "Master Workshop" (working range of the analysis team) and "assembly line" (automatic targeting) are in the existing architecture of a company included in a way that the environment and its benefits can be used as far as possible. This includes especially all tasks around data preparations.

In general: All the developed models will be passed as a code / script and archived in an archive, including its metadata and also about their use. The application of models based on the scripts is the final step of the calculation of variables at the end of a session or a slot. For each active model the prediction is calculated as relevant forecast value per unique client (UC) and is stored in a separate variable and made available to the Target Builder.

In the Target Builder (an instrument for targeted delivery of content), these predictive capabilities of profiles are used to provide target audiences for online campaigns and make them ready to be marked. So every user with fitting profile is addressed.

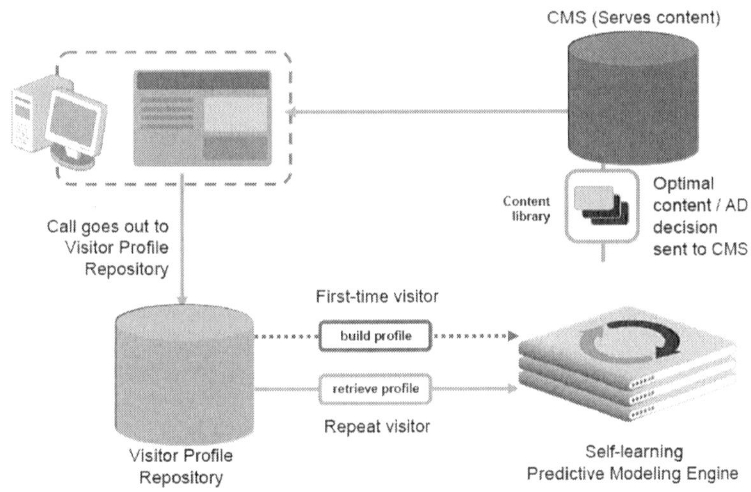

Fig. 2. Automatic Predictive Targeting

3.3 Data flows and database

The bases for all analyses are the behavior data of the UC on the respective websites. Ideally the behavior data can be enriched by information from questioning or login data. One can differentiate between standard/general behavior and/or interest-conditioned information These profile and behavior data per UC are computed relative to different time windows. Both are formed from large numbers of variables. The variables should reflect different views on the UC.

In the context of the modelling in the assembly line, only an examined subset of variables is used, in order to grant stability, robustness and performance essential for automation. That can be seen somehow as the standard dataset. The size and content of it is the outcome of experience and domain knowledge obtainable from the analyses team. Using the Pareto principle the dataset should contain roughly 20 % of all potential data to be the basis of 80% of all easy prediction problems. To ensure that data preparation fits the time constraints of the Assembly line, it is important to use optimization techniques that help to deliver the data as fast as possible. After the structure of standard dataset is defined and adjusted, it will be created fully automatically by the systems.

As in other industrial processes it is important to identify and separate different process steps, such as data handling and calculations so that they can be standardized and optimized to deliver an outcome of reliable quality and with a more or less small standard error. About the data preparation including all necessary (automatically done) transformations, it lead us to the fact we should choose robust methods that will help to generate data that fits most (modeling) situations but might not be the optimal one for every single case as you would get, when you do the analytics by hand through an expert in your company. Where you try to optimize the modeling result by doing a constant looping out of data preparation, analytics and measurement, especially under time constraints, this looping has to be at a minimum.

An essential part of the daily profile building step is data preparation. It is needed both for the modeling / verification as well as for the application of existing scores. All of has to be done in a time-critical area.

So that modeling or deployment can take place in the current session, it is indispensable that the session data can be accessed at any time in the session.

To train and validate a model, very fast sampling is mandatory. Please keep in mind that the relation between those who act (target=1) and those who do not act (target=0) is very unbalanced. It is very likely that you have just 500 UC acting and 5 million UC not acting. As part of the modeling issue, it makes a big difference in calculation time whether you have to calculate slightly more than 5 million records or just a couple of hundred. So if you start to build an assembly line it is required to work out and test a sampling strategy that best suits your individual situation.

3.4 Modelling Aspects

Similar to the data preparation, the assembly line needs for its modeling engine a data mining algorithm that will deliver good and stable models without any interaction with an expert. The algorithm should be fast and the time needed for the deployment of models should be as small as possible, especially if it is planned to use the assembly line for nearly real time forecasting. If it is under business reason not so important to be real time, for example it is enough if you use the data of the last finished session as the newest one to be included in the forecasting, or as a base forecast that is shaped by the content click on or searched for, then the time for modeling and deployment might not be so time critical. Based on many tests simulating the situation like an assembly line, out of all the algorithms, the family of decision trees wins most, and delivers fast very good results.

The fully automated quality control is the next step in the process to deal with; the task here is to define the small border between not "quite as good" and "good enough under business reason". If your expectations for the modelling quality are too high you will end up with lots of models transferred back from assembly line to workshop to be redone by the experts, so you will lose time and it will cost you more money to produce the models. If your quality is too low you will lose business, e.g. lower click rates.

In quality control we are looking after new (freshly developed) models as well as after models that have been in duty for a while, so the chosen quality control process and it measurements must be able to do a constant quality control on all active models to notice in time when a model needs refreshment.

3.5 Challenges and critical success factors

The complexity of the process of fully automated predictive targeting and modeling of real-time online conduct presents some statistical challenges: During sampling the minimum reasonable number of events = 1 (e.g. clicks), stratification, sampling routines has to be fixed sensitively. Forecasting methods are judged in terms of prediction quality, stability, development, etc. Performance, durability, run-time behavior, parameterization, and automation of error detection must be considered in the selection of quality assurance methods.

Similarly, critical success factors should not be ignored: Are uncontrollable optimization steps / algorithms influencing the ad server that originally predicted massive click behavior? Are tags are missing in the banner? Are there so few clicks that it takes too long to get a critical mass for modeling?

4 Results

Fully automatic targeting and predictive modeling of real-time online behavior are at the very beginning of their development and are valuable tools provided critical success factors and requirements are carefully observed in the implementation and the environment. All being well we can obtain fully automated predictive targeting even based literally on the last click in real time, and these predictions can be flexible and up to date. This allows rapid response to changes and trends in the rapidly changing online marketplace.

References

1. Alberto Messina et all: A generalised cross-modal clustering method applied to multimedia news semantic indexing and retrieval, Juan Quemada et all (Ed.), Proceedings of the 18th International Conference on World Wide Web, WWW 2009, Madrid, 2009
2. Alice Klever: Behavioural Targeting: An Online Analysis for Efficient Media Planning?, Diplomica, 2009
3. Andrea Ahlemeyer-Stubbe: Behavioral Targeting: Which Method produces the most Robust Prediction? A Confrontation between Decisions Trees, Neural Networks and Regressions, Petra Perner (Ed.): Advances in Data Mining. 9th Industrial Conference, ICDM 2008, Ibai Publishing, 2009
4. Andrea Ahlemeyer-Stubbe: Predictive Targeting: Buzzword or Reality - The potential of Automatic Behavioral Targeted Advertising in Online Marketing, Petra Perner (Ed.), Advances in Data Mining. 9th Industrial Conference, ICDM 2008, Ibai Publishing, 2009

5. David S.Evans:, The Online Advertising Industry: Economics, Evolution, and Privacy, The Journal of Economic Perspectives, Volume 23, Number 3, Summer 2009 , pp. 37-60(24), 2009
6. Deepak Agarwal et all: Spatio-temporal models for estimating click-through rate, Juan Quemada et all (Ed.), Proceedings of the 18th International Conference on World Wide Web, WWW 2009, Madrid, 2009
7. Foster J. Provost et all: Data acquisition and cost-effective predictive modeling: targeting offers for electronic commerce, Maria L. Gini et all (Ed)., Proceedings of the 9th International Conference on Electronic Commerce: The Wireless World of Electronic Commerce, 2007, Minneapolis, 2007
8. Internet World Stats 2011, http://www.internetworldstats.com/stats4.htm, 25.September 2011
9. Joseph Reisinger, Marius Pasca: Bootstrapped extraction of class attributes. Juan Quemada et al (Ed.), Proceedings of the 18th International Conference on World Wide Web, WWW 2009, Madrid, 2009
10. Jun Yan, et al: How much can behavioral targeting help online advertising?, Juan Quemada et all (Ed.), Proceedings of the 18th International Conference on World Wide Web, WWW 2009, Madrid, 2009
11. OVK Online-Report 2011/01, Online-Vermarkterkreis(OVK) im Bundesverband Digitale Wirtschaft (BVDW) e.V., (Hrsg), Düsseldorf, 2011
12. P. Perner, Case-based reasoning and the statistical challenges, Journal Quality and Reliability Engineering International Volume 24 Issue 6 (October 2008), p 705-720.
13. Petra Perner, G. Fiss: Intelligent E-marketing with Web Mining, Personalization, and User-Adpated Interfaces, Petra Perner (Ed.), Advances in Data Mining, Applications in E-Commerce, Medicine, and Knowledge Management [Industrial Conference on Data Mining, Leipzig, Germany, June 2002]. Lecture Notes in Computer Science, Springer 2002
14. M. Reichle, P. Perner, K.-D. Althoff, Data Preparation of Web Log Files for Marketing Aspects Analyses, In: Petra Perner (Ed.): Advances in Data Mining, Applications in Medicine, Web Mining, Marketing, Image and Signal Mining, lncs 4065, Springer 2006,p. 131-145.

Author Index

Announcement

World Congress DSA 2020
The Frontiers in Intelligent Data and Signal Analysis
July 12 - 23, 2020, New York, USA

www.worldcongressdsa.com

We are inviting you to our fourth World congress on the Frontiers of Signal and Image Analysis DSA 2020 to New York, Germany.

This congress will feature three events:

- the 16th International Conference on Machine Learning and Data Mining MLDM (www.mldm.de),
- the 20th Industrial Conference on Data Mining ICDM (www.data-mining-forum.de),
- and the 15th International Conference on Mass Data Analysis of Signals and Images in Artificial Intelligence&Pattern Recognition MDA-AI&PR (www.mda-signals.de).

Workshops and Tutorial will also be given.

Come to join us to the most exciting event on Intelligent Data and Signal Analysis.

Sincerely your,
Prof. Dr. Petra Perner

MLDM www.mldm.de
icdm www.data-mining-forum.de
mda www.mda-signals.de

Transactions on Mass-Data Analysis of Images and Signals

(ISSN:1868-6451)

The International Journal "Transactions on Mass-Data Analysis of Images and Signals" is a periodical appearing once a year.

The automatic analysis of images and signals in medicine, biotechnology, and chemistry is a challenging and demanding field. Signal-producing procedures by microscopes, spectrometers and other sensors have found their way into wide fields of medicine, biotechnology, economy and environmental analysis. With this arises the problem of the automatic mass analysis of signal information. Signal-interpreting systems which generate automatically the desired target statements from the signals are therefore of compelling necessity. The continuation of mass analyses on the basis of the classical procedures leads to investments of proportions that are not feasible. New procedures and system architectures are therefore required.

Net Price (per issue): EURO 100
Germany (per issue): EURO 107 (incl. 7% VAT)

Submission for the journal should be send to:
info@ibai-publishing.org

For more information visited: www.ibai-publishing.org/journal/massdata/about.php

ibai-publishing
Arno-Nitzsche-Str. 45
04277 Leipzig, Germany

CURRAN ASSOCIATES INC.
proceedings.com

ISBN 978-1-5108-9515-7
9 781510 895157

84th Conference of the New Zealand Society of Animal Production (NZSAP 2024)

Proceedings of the New Zealand Society of Animal Production
Volume 84

Omaru, New Zealand
5-7 November 2024

NZSAP